# BATCH COOKING

## Save Time, Save Money!

WHITE STAR PUBLISHERS

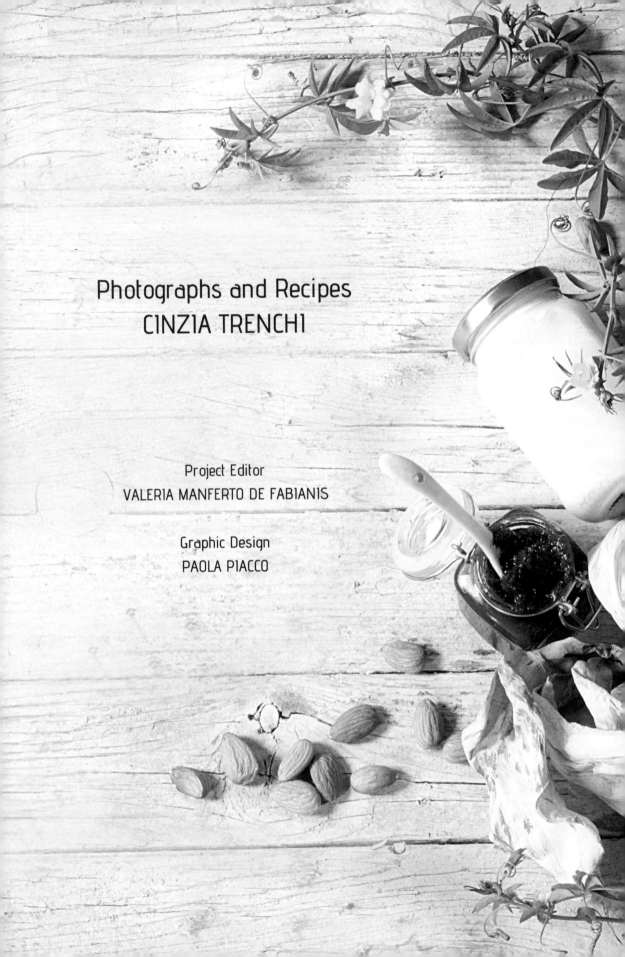

Photographs and Recipes
CINZIA TRENCHI

Project Editor
VALERIA MANFERTO DE FABIANIS

Graphic Design
PAOLA PIACCO

# Contents

# Introduction

Paying attention to what we eat is becoming a necessity, but adapting can be an enormous pleasure! In addition to being a core part of self-care, cooking is also fun and creative, and it allows you to have control over your food, the safety of the dishes you eat, and the quality of the chosen ingredients.

Batch cooking is a meal planning system that involves preparing a week's worth of meals — for eating at home or out — in just a few hours, to then store in the refrigerator, freezer, or pantry.

Of course, it takes a lot of organization to avoid going to a restaurant, café, or bar to eat. You need to build a collection of accessories and basic ingredients, which will allow you to optimize your time, so that you can prepare dishes for the whole week.

This means that, instead of doing small shops every now and then, you will have to prepare a complete list for one weekly shop. It is also important that you buy a few accessories to help you and that you have enough containers to store the food you have prepared.

The objectives to work toward are choosing organic food and seasonal vegetables, with zero-food mileage, in order to discover the world behind a dish, which we often eat in a hurry during our lunch break. Furthermore, you may be surprised to learn that our food choices can promote not only our health but also the protection of the planet and that recycled plastic food packaging can contribute to our lives having less impact on the environment.

Batch cooking also helps you to become familiar with both food preservation and the reduction of waste, which often also concerns the containers that pass through our homes, such as bottles, jars, and boxes.

All glass containers can be reused indefinitely. To vacuum seal them, simply replace the lid, and they are then ready to perfectly preserve drinks and juices. Glass jars can be used to organize the pantry or stock up on things that many stores are now selling without packaging, as well as for storing your homemade jams, soups, and condiments. Cardboard and tin boxes can also be useful containers for storing cookies, cakes, bread, and breadsticks. Your pantry will gradually become a familiar place, where you can find the resources you need to organize your meal planning.

And what about plastic wrap? The one we use to wrap, cover, and protect food?

Let's use it less and less in favor of silicone stretch lids, for example, or certified airtight containers that are recycled and safe for storing food. While they may cost more than generic products, they are often suitable for using in the microwave, have air valve lids, and are designed for vacuum packing.

While we're on the subject of vacuum packing, buying a vacuum sealer is worth the small investment (they can cost anywhere from around $30 upward) because you can be sure that your food will have a long, healthy, and protected shelf life. There are only a few things vacuum packing is not suitable for: foods with a high water content or soft foods, because the removal of air will squash them. But with a little practice, you will have no difficulty choosing the right storage system.

So, how much time do we have to invest to prepare a week's worth of meals, after you have organized the shopping, a well-stocked pantry, and a good collection of accessories? You'll also need to put aside half a day every weekend. So, is it worth it?

Yes, it is — for many reasons, the first being our health. Medicine is focusing more and more attention on the possible negative or positive consequences of our diet and relative quality of life. Then, there is the certainty of eating foods prepared with carefully selected, high-quality ingredients, cooked with care and love! Planning is necessary, of course: in addition to a detailed shopping list, the fridge and freezer must be organized, as the various shelves and containers will be used to store the meals for the different days of the week. It is best to use lighter and more easily transportable plastic containers for meals that you take to work, and glass containers for meals you will eat at home.

This book contains 68 recipes, accompanied by original photos, for making easy dishes to organize your meals with, from breakfast to an aperitif with friends, and, of course, lunch and dinner. You can plan your week by browsing through the various recipes, basing your choices on the season and your personal tastes in food. Once you get into the habit, you can start making larger quantities, producing several meals from your favorite recipe, or inviting friends to dinner at the last minute.

The recipes are divided into four weeks, from which you can draw inspiration to prepare breakfast, snacks, individual portions, or nibbles for an aperitif. By investing just a little of your time, you will have the certainty of eating food that has been made with care and attention, not only for your personal health but also for the environment.

# PLASTIC CONTAINERS

Whatever their size or color, plastic containers are extremely practical, light, and durable. They can be found in a variety of sizes suitable for very small to large quantities of liquid and solid foods, and they are also safe for use in the freezer and the microwave.

They are an excellent solution for organizing your refrigerator so that you can store meals, flowers for decorating dishes, fragrant herbs, sauces, and condiments for several days.

But be careful when buying them, because there are containers that as well as not being eco-friendly are also of poor quality.

Before choosing, take a few minutes to read the label: in particular, the material it is made of, the temperatures it can withstand, and if it can be used in the microwave.

It is best to use recycled plastic containers, which, unlike glass, should be replaced when they start to show signs of wear.

## GLASS CONTAINERS

Glass is the material par excellence for food storage containers. Glass containers are sterile, infinitely reusable, and transparent, and they come in all shapes and sizes — definitely an exceptional addition to our kitchen.

Furthermore, we can reuse (for free!) all the glass jars we already have lying around, such as those that contained ready-made sauces from the store or the ones we bought for homemade jellies and fruit juices we never got around to making. These containers are ideal for helping us to organize our pantry and should never be thrown away. Once you have washed them thoroughly and removed the labels, you can use them indefinitely for soups, juices, broths, and sauces. As long as the lid is screwed on tight, food will stay fresh in the refrigerator for a few days and can then be heated directly over a bain-marie or transferred to a pan.

And if you want to make a large batch of something, such as pickled vegetables or jelly because you have a lot of fruit and veg from the garden, all you need to do to preserve them correctly is put a new lid on your glass containers and vacuum seal them by boiling the jars or bottles for 20 minutes.

# CONTAINERS WITH AIR VALVE LIDS

In addition to paying attention to recycled materials that have a minimum impact on the environment, when choosing your containers you should also take into consideration the appliances you use the most and opt for those that can be used in the microwave, oven, dishwasher, and so on. These specific appliances can be extremely helpful in your meal planning.

Therefore, you can buy hermetically sealed containers with air valve lids for the microwave or glass containers that can be kept in the refrigerator and then put in the oven, if you prefer to use a traditional oven. And if you like natural materials, there are containers with bamboo lids that have adjustable seals for vacuum sealing.

# SILICONE STRETCH LIDS

These are a practical and safe solution to preserving and protecting food without using the usual plastic wrap, and in fact, thanks to their flexibility, they have done an excellent job of replacing it almost completely. Whether you want to cover half a melon or a jug of fruit juice, their versatility allows you to use them directly on the fruit or original container, avoiding both transferring food and the use of special containers. In addition to being extremely practical and safe, they can also be used in the microwave, refrigerator, freezer, and dishwasher.

Furthermore, these lids also help reduce the use of plastic because, by adapting perfectly to even half a lemon, there is less and less need for bags, plastic wrap, and containers. They are generally found in packs of six containing the most common sizes, and they can be used on any type of surface, from fruit and vegetables to tableware, pans, and various utensils.

# VACUUM PACKING

With a vacuum sealer, it is possible to extract almost all of the air from the bag, and — thanks to the removal of the oxygen — the oxidation process slows down, maintaining the freshness of the food. This technique can be used for most cooked and raw foods.

In addition to being easier to store in the pantry (especially seeds, flours, etc.), our bags of vacuum-packed food can also be kept in the refrigerator or freezer for long periods of time.

Vacuum sealers come in a range of sizes, and the price can vary greatly. For home use, the most important characteristics are undoubtedly lightness, size, and ease of use. It is also important to choose the right bags, as they have different characteristics: some can be used to store food at room temperature, or in the refrigerator or freezer, while others can also be used to cook the food.

When buying the bags for your vacuum sealer, it is important to dedicate the necessary time to check the quality, characteristics, and integrity.

# FOOD WRAPS, PARCHMENT PAPER, AND VACUUM-SEALED BAGS

No kitchen should be without parchment paper, which is essential, for example, for making cakes with a compact base that is easy to transfer from the baking tray to the serving plate. It is also useful for cooking food without sauces. It can be white or hazelnut-colored, and it's a good idea to check the instructions on the package at the time of purchase to see what temperature it can be exposed to without any consequences.

Tin or aluminum foil is adaptable and easy to use, and is a valid aid for cooking food in the oven and protecting our food. Although there has been a lot of talk about metals contaminating food, there is no proof of this being the case for aluminum foil.

Plastic wrap is perfect for wrapping and protecting food, even if studies on the possible contamination of food have been ongoing for years. It's best to buy one that isn't too sticky and that has less impact on the environment and food.

Bags for vacuum packing and storing food are the perfect accessory for our "food planning": they adapt to our needs and are an excellent way to save space when storing food in the pantry or freezer, at the same time keeping the contents fresh. Always make sure that they are sustainable and eco-friendly.

# Week 1

If you are already an experienced cook, learning how to batch cook will be a breeze. If you're not, the first tip is to get a notebook and write down all the ingredients you need, your chosen recipes, and how long they take to make. Furthermore, to save time, it's always better to start with longer recipes, or those that require breaks (like leavening or cooling time), and to make and cook several dishes at the same time.

If you are using dried legumes that need soaking, you need to do that the night before, and it is also important to remember to take the meal out of the freezer and put it into the refrigerator 24 hours before serving. If this is your first time batch cooking, organizing your ingredients will be a big help because it will make your cooking experience much easier. It is very important that all the various foods in your pantry are placed in different containers, possibly labeled and divided into categories: all the herbs in small jars on one side; dried fruit, flours, legumes, and seeds in glass containers; washed vegetables, dried vegetables, meats, fish, and cheeses in airtight containers in the refrigerator.

This little trick allows you to have everything you need easily at hand, and if you always use the same containers, stored in the same position, it will be easy and quick to find them. After you have transferred the food you've made into vacuum-sealed bags, airtight jars, or containers, it is useful to immediately attach removable labels indicating the date it was made and the contents.

# WHOLE WHEAT CHOCOLATE AND HAZELNUT CROISSANTS

4

Easy

10 minutes

20 minutes

- 9 oz (250 g) rectangular sheet of ready-made whole wheat puff pastry
- 2 tbsp (40 g) jelly of your choice
- 1 egg yolk
- 2.8 oz (80 g) dark chocolate
- 2 3/4 tbsp (20 g) chopped hazelnuts

Preheat the oven to 350°F (180°C).

Melt the chocolate over a bain-marie.

Cut the puff pastry into 4 triangles, place a spoonful of jelly in the center of each triangle, then roll into the shape of a croissant. Put them on a baking tray lined with parchment paper, mix the egg yolk with a pastry brush, and brush the top of the croissants.

Cook in the oven for about 20 minutes, checking every now and then that they are not burning. Take out of the oven and leave to cool for a few minutes. Cover with a few tablespoons of chocolate, sprinkle with the chopped hazelnuts, and leave to cool.

Put the croissants in a rigid container from which you can remove the air, and then keep in the refrigerator. Leave at room temperature for a few hours before serving.

7 days
in the fridge

# MINI FOCACCIA FILLED WITH BLACKBERRY JELLY

4

Easy

20 minutes

60 minutes

6 days
and over

- 7 cups (1 kg) blackberries
- 1 1/4 tsp (5 g) agar-agar
- 1/2 cup (100 g) granulated sugar
- 14 oz (400 g) ready-made dough
- 1/2 cup (100 g) peanut oil
- powdered sugar

Trim the blackberries and boil them in 1 cup (1/4 l) of water for 30 minutes over low heat, then use a food mill to separate the seeds from the flesh. Put the flesh back in the pan with the sugar and agar-agar. Thicken over low heat, stirring every now and then. After about 30 minutes, remove from the heat and pour into jars while still hot, then put the lids on.

Roll the dough out to a thickness of about 0.1 in (3 mm) and make it level. Cut out discs, divide the jelly between them, then fold them in half. Make sure the edges are firmly closed.

Heat the oil to 325°F (170°C), and fry each focaccia for a minute on each side. Once cooked, put them on a paper towel. When the focaccia are cold, put them in a well-sealed container. Before serving, put them on a baking tray and heat in the oven for 10 minutes at 125°F (50°C), then sprinkle with powdered sugar.

If vacuum-sealed, blackberry jam can be kept for a very long time, even months.

## APPLE FRITTERS

2

Medium

20 minutes

20 minutes

2 days
in the fridge

- 2 1/4 cups (200 g) all-purpose flour
- 2 egg yolks
- 3 tbsp milk
- 1 tsp (2 g) cake yeast
- 1 apple
- 2/5 cup (50 g) powdered sugar

Mix the flour with the egg yolks, yeast, and 3 tablespoons of milk, until the dough is smooth and lump-free. Roll it out, and cut out an even number of discs.

Peel the apple and cut it into thin slices. Cover half of the discs with apple, cover them with the remaining discs, and make a hole in the middle with a small ring mold. To seal them, press the inner and outer edges firmly with your fingers.

Preheat the oven to 350°F (180°C). Put the fritters on a baking tray lined with parchment paper, and cook for 20 minutes. When they have risen well and turned golden brown, take out of the oven, leave to cool, and put in a container. Keep in the refrigerator.

Sprinkle with powdered sugar before serving.

BREAKFAST

## LEMON AND CHOCOLATE SEMOLINA SLICES WITH ALMOND MILK

4

Easy

5 minutes

10 minutes

4 days
in the fridge

- 4 1/4 cups (1 l) milk
- 1 1/2 cups (250 g) semolina
- 3 tbsp (30 g) unsweetened cocoa powder
- the zest of 1 lemon
- 1/4 cup (50 g) granulated sugar

Divide the semolina between two pans: 1 cup (150 g) in one, 1/2 cup (100 g) in the other; add the cocoa powder to the latter.

Add the lemon zest to the white semolina, and divide the sugar and milk equally between the two pans. Bring both pans to a boil, stirring the semolina continuously. Boil for about 3 minutes, then pour the mixtures into two airtight containers with a diameter of about 6–8 in (15–20 cm).

When the semolina is cold, cover and put in the refrigerator. Before serving, cut into pieces and leave at room temperature for a couple of hours.

# CHERRY JELLY MUFFINS

4

Easy

5 minutes

- 2 1/4 cups (200 g) all-purpose flour
- 3 1/2 tbsp (50 g) melted butter
- 1 egg
- 1/4 cup (50 g) granulated sugar
- 1/2 cup (100 g) yogurt
- 3 tbsp (40 g) milk
- 1 tsp (2 g) cake yeast
- 1/2 cup (100 g) cherry jelly

20 minutes

Mix the sugar, flour, and yeast in a bowl. Stir in the egg, yogurt, milk, and melted butter. When the mixture is smooth, add all the dry ingredients and mix again.

up to
5 days

Preheat the oven to 350°F (180°C), line the muffin pan with paper muffin cups, and fill each one halfway. Add a teaspoon of jelly to each one, then put in the oven. After about 20 minutes, use a toothpick to check if they are cooked: if it comes out clean, they're ready. Take them out of the oven, and leave to cool.

Wrap the muffins in tissue paper or parchment paper, and put them in a container with a lid.

You can revive them by warming them in the oven before serving.

BREAKFAST

# CHOCOLATE MOUSSE WITH CHOPPED HAZELNUTS

2

Easy

10 minutes

5 minutes

1 day
in the fridge

- 3/4 cup (2 dl) milk
- 1.7 oz (50 g) dark chocolate
- 1 tbsp corn starch
- 2 1/2 tbsp (30 g) granulated sugar
- chopped hazelnuts

Heat the corn starch, sugar, and chopped chocolate in a pan, then dilute with the milk until the mixture is smooth and creamy. Bring to a boil, stirring continuously. Pour into cups, leave to cool, cover, and put in the refrigerator.

Take the mousses out the refrigerator just before serving, sprinkle with the chopped hazelnuts, and serve.

BREAKFAST

# GREEN TEA AND ALMOND MILK BLANCMANGE

4

Easy

5 minutes

- 2 1/4 cups (5 dl) milk
- 4 1/4 tbsp (30 g) corn starch
- 1/4 cup (50 g) granulated sugar
- 3 tbsp (20 g) green tea powder
- 2 tbsp (10 g) sliced almonds
- 0.7 oz (20 g) dark chocolate

5 minutes

3 days
in the fridge

Melt the chocolate over a bain-marie, and keep it melted until you are ready to use it. In a pan, heat the sugar, corn starch, and green tea, dilute with the milk, and bring to a boil. Leave to boil for 2 minutes, stirring continuously, and then pour into containers.

You can use glass jars with a lid or aluminum molds, depending on whether you are going to eat them at home or not. Decorate them with the chocolate sauce and sliced almonds, put the lid on or cover with foil, and keep them in the refrigerator until you are ready to eat them.

# WHOLE WHEAT PASTA WITH CHERRY TOMATOES AND CAPERS

2

Easy

5 minutes

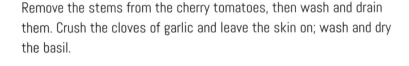

10 minutes

3 days
in the fridge

- 7 oz (200 g) whole wheat pasta
- 4 cups (600 g) different-colored cherry tomatoes
- 1 tbsp capers with their salt
- 2 garlic cloves
- basil to taste
- 4 tbsp oil
- salt and pepper

Remove the stems from the cherry tomatoes, then wash and drain them. Crush the cloves of garlic and leave the skin on; wash and dry the basil.

Bring a generous amount of unsalted water to a boil. Put the oil, capers with their salt, and garlic in a large frying pan, and cook for one minute over high heat. Add the cherry tomatoes, stir, and squash a few of them. Turn off after 5 minutes, add the basil, and cover. Cook the pasta for 2–3 minutes less than the time indicated on the packet, drain, put under cold water to stop the pasta from cooking further, and then pour into the frying pan with the sauce.
Mix thoroughly, and put in a vacuum storage container.

You can keep it in the refrigerator for 3 days. Cook over high heat for a couple of minutes before serving.

If you want to put some of the sauce to one side, fill a 9 oz (250 g) jar, put the lid on, and — if you want to sterilize it — boil it for 20 minutes. Now you have an emergency sauce for pasta, rice, millet, etc.

INDIVIDUAL PORTIONS

# BASMATI RICE WITH MUSHROOM SAUCE

2

Easy

5 minutes

- 1/2 cup (100 g) basmati rice
- 2 cups (200 g) seasonal mushrooms of your choice
- 1/2 cup (20 g) parsley
- 2 sprigs of thyme
- 2 tbsp (30 g) butter
- 2 tbsp extra virgin olive oil
- 1 clove of garlic
- 2 1/4 cups (0.5 l) vegetable stock
- salt and pepper

10 minutes

Trim, wash, and dry the mushrooms, then slice them.
Trim the parsley and thyme, and finely chop them. Peel and chop the garlic.

2 days
in the fridge

Melt the butter in the oil, fry the garlic, and add half the mushrooms. Mix, then add the rice. Cook for about 4 minutes, adding hot stock when necessary, then add the remaining mushrooms. Continue cooking for another 6 minutes, then turn off, add salt and pepper, and transfer the rice into an airtight glass container.

Thanks to the heat, the lid is sucked down, creating a vacuum: this allows you to keep it safely in the refrigerator.

Before serving, you can heat the rice directly in the jar over a bain-marie or in a frying pan with a little oil.

INDIVIDUAL PORTIONS

# GINGER CHICKEN WITH ZUCCHINI
# AND BELL PEPPER

4

Easy

5 minutes

- 1 lb (500 g) chicken breast
- 2 round zucchinis
- 4 round bell peppers
- 1 tbsp ground turmeric
- 1 tsp grated ginger
- 2 tbsp extra virgin olive oil
- salt and pepper

10 minutes

Dissolve the turmeric in two tablespoons of water. Trim the vegetables and cut them into thin rounds. Cut the chicken into strips.

Pour the oil into a large frying pan, add the chicken, vegetables, and ginger, then stir. As soon as the ingredients are dry, add the turmeric water. Cook over medium heat for a few minutes, stirring continuously. If necessary, add a tablespoon of water every now and then. Add salt and pepper to taste. After about 7 minutes, check to see if it has reached the desired consistency.

7 days
in the fridge

Take off the heat, pour into a hot glass container, put the lid on, leave to cool, and then put in the refrigerator.

If you heat the glass container in the oven or boiling water, and the contents are very hot, a vacuum should usually form. This will allow you to preserve the dish without any problems.

INDIVIDUAL PORTIONS

# STUFFED ARTICHOKES

2

Easy

10 minutes

10–12 minutes

1 day
in the fridge

- 4 artichokes
- 3/4 cup (200 g) ricotta
- 1/2 cup (50 g) grated Parmigiano Reggiano
- 1 tbsp chopped dried aromatic herbs (rosemary, sage, etc.)
- 4 tbsp extra virgin olive oil
- salt and pepper

Mix the herbs with the ricotta and half the Parmigiano Reggiano. Add salt and pepper to taste. Trim the artichokes, cut off any sharp spines, and trim the stems. Scoop out the middle for the filling. Divide the filling between the artichokes, press it down, and sprinkle with a little Parmigiano Reggiano.

Put the oil in a small pan and arrange the artichokes so that they are standing up straight, then cook over high heat with the lid on. Turn the artichokes upside down after about 5–6 minutes, cook for another 3 minutes, and then turn them back over. Add salt, leave to cook for a few more minutes, then remove from the heat and leave to cool.

Keep in the refrigerator, in an oven safe glass container.

INDIVIDUAL PORTIONS

# BEAN, PUMPKIN, AND MILLET SOUP

4

Easy

15 minutes

- 1 1/2 cups (300 g) mixed dried beans of your choice
- 7 oz (200 g) pumpkin, cut into pieces
- 2 1/2 tbsp (30 g) millet
- 1 tsp chopped dried rosemary
- 1 onion
- 1 stick of celery
- 1 tbsp tomato paste
- salt and pepper

70–80 minutes

Soak the beans overnight, then wash and drain them. Trim and slice the onion, celery, and rosemary, then put them in a pan with the millet, pumpkin, beans, and 6 1/4 cups (1.5 l) of water.

5 days
in the fridge

Boil over high heat for one hour, checking that too much water isn't evaporating, and adding more if necessary. Halfway through cooking, add the tomato paste and check the consistency of the beans; add salt and pepper to taste.

When the legumes are soft, take off the heat and transfer to a hot jar, put the lid on, and leave to cool. It should usually vacuum seal (the lid is sucked down onto the jar, and — if the lid has a rubber ring inside — it should remain closed even when unhooked).

In this way, you can eat the soup up to 5 days after you have made it.

Before serving, you can heat the soup directly in the glass container, and then serve with crusty bread.

# GREEN BORAGE LEAF AND POTATO SOUP

4

Easy

10 minutes

30 minutes

6 days
in the fridge

- 6 1/2 cups (200 g) borage leaves
- 2 potatoes
- 1 white onion
- salt and pepper
- 2 tbsp oil (optional)
- stale bread (optional)

Trim the borage leaves, peel the potatoes and onion, and chop all the ingredients.

Cook for 30 minutes in 4 1/4 cups (1 l) of boiling water, with the lid on, and then blend.

Leave to cool, and then transfer to a freezer safe container. Put the lid on and put in the freezer.

Take it out of the freezer the night before you need it, and leave it to defrost in the refrigerator. Heat it in a pan, and — if you like — serve with a drizzle of oil and slices of stale bread.

# BASMATI RICE WITH CLAMS AND CHERRY TOMATOES

2

Easy

10 minutes

8 minutes

1 day
in the fridge

- 1/2 cup (100 g) basmati rice
- 18 oz (500 g) clams
- 1 tbsp chopped parsley and fennel fronds
- 8 cherry tomatoes
- 4 tbsp extra virgin olive oil
- salt and pepper

Wash the clams and leave them to open in a frying pan over high heat, without adding any liquid: it will take 2–3 minutes for the valves to open. Drain the clam juice, and put it to one side for cooking the rice.

Heat 4 1/4 cups (1 l) of water, which you will need for cooking the rice. Wash the cherry tomatoes, and cut them in half.

Remove half of the shell from each clam. Fry the oil and herbs in a non-stick frying pan, add the rice, and toast it for a few seconds. Add the clam stock, and then gradually add the water when necessary, using a ladle. After about 7–8 minutes, add the clams, cherry tomatoes, salt, and pepper, then taste to check the consistency of the rice (cook it a few minutes less than the time indicated on the packet, so it isn't overcooked the next day).

Take off the heat, and divide between two glass containers with a lid. Leave to cool before putting the lid on, and keep in the refrigerator until you are ready to eat it.

INDIVIDUAL PORTIONS

# GREEN AND RED SPREAD WITH TURMERIC BREAD

4

Easy

10 minutes

**For the green spread:**
- 13 tbsp (50 g) trimmed parsley
- 1 clove of garlic
- 4 tbsp extra virgin olive oil
- 2 1/2 tbsp (20 g) fresh breadcrumbs
- 1 tbsp apple cider vinegar
- salt and pepper

- Turmeric bread

**For the red spread:**
- 1 3/4 cups (300 g) ripe cherry tomatoes
- 1 tsp harissa chili paste
- 1 tbsp granulated sugar
- 1 tsp vinegar
- 4 tbsp extra virgin olive oil
- salt and pepper

5 minutes

4 days

Slice and toast the bread. Leave to cool, and then vacuum pack it.

Chop the parsley and garlic, and soak the breadcrumbs in the apple cider vinegar. Add the breadcrumbs to the chopped parsley and garlic, and mix thoroughly. Put the mixture into a bowl, add the oil, and salt and pepper to taste. Transfer to a jar with a lid.

Wash the cherry tomatoes, and put in a frying pan with the sugar; when the sugar has dissolved, add the harissa and the vinegar. Stir over high heat for a couple of minutes, then add salt and pepper to taste. Remove from the heat, leave to cool, add the oil, and transfer to a jar with a lid.

Before serving, warm the bread in the oven at 200°F (100°C) for 5 minutes, and top with the spreads.

# MINI CHEESE PIZZAS WITH SUN-DRIED TOMATOES AND BLACK SESAME SEEDS

4

Easy

10 minutes

- 9 oz (250 g) ready-made puff pastry
- 2 oz (50 g) soft cheese, such as Toma
- 10 sun-dried tomatoes in oil
- 2 tbsp (20 g) black sesame seeds

10 minutes

2 days
in the fridge

Preheat the oven to 400°F (200°C).

Cut the cheese into small pieces. Chop the tomatoes, roll out the pastry, and cut out discs using a 2.5–3 in (6–7 cm) ring mold. Place them on a baking tray lined with parchment paper, and top with the cheese and tomatoes. Finally, sprinkle them with sesame seeds. Cook for 8–10 minutes, checking every now and then that they are not burning.

Take out of the oven, and leave to cool. Put them in a container, put the lid on, and keep in the refrigerator.

Before serving, heat them in the oven at 400°F (200°C) for 2–3 minutes.

SNACKS

# CHICKPEA FLOUR PANCAKES WITH BELL PEPPER

2

Easy

10 minutes

10 minutes

- 3/4 cup (100 g) chickpea flour
- 2 eggs
- 1/4 bell pepper, scraped
- 4 tbsp (10 g) chopped parsley
- 2 tbsp peanut oil

Chop the bell pepper. Mix the chickpea flour with the eggs, pour in a little cold water, and mix until the batter is smooth and lump-free. Add the parsley and chopped bell pepper.

Cover a 4–5 in (10–12 cm) frying pan with the peanut oil, using a paper towel. Pour in a ladleful of the chickpea batter, and cook until it is firm and comes away from the pan. Turn the pancake over, and cook in the same way. Repeat until you have used all the batter.

Leave to cool, put the pancakes in a vacuum storage container, and keep in the refrigerator until you are ready to use them.

You can keep aromatic herbs (and leaf vegetables) for several days: just wash and drain them, wrap them in a paper towel, and put them in a container with the lid on, letting as much air out as possible. Keep them in the refrigerator until you need them.

5 days
in the fridge

SNACKS

# Week 2

Batch cooking involves preserving food without the use of additives and tries to make the most of the intrinsic properties of the ingredients, respecting the past tradition of stocking up on our supply of fruit and vegetables in the summer, in preparation for winter, when nature rests and doesn't provide us with anything. Thanks to greenhouses and transport, today we can find everything in the stores year-round, even if the price in terms of environmental impact is very high: the only way to offer consumers fruit and veg that look good and appetizing is to use chemical preservatives and additives. So, what exactly is the point of meal planning?

Firstly, we have far more choice. We can decide what we want to eat, opt to follow the seasons, and choose the quality of the food we buy, where it was produced, and — last but not least — how much we spend. Ready meals can certainly be tasty, practical, quick to prepare, and great as an occasional solution, but they cost much more than those we make ourselves.

Homemade meals allow you to follow a specific diet, based on your taste or particular requirements. Furthermore, meal planning allows you to choose the basic ingredients — oil, salt, condiments in general — and, above all, makes it possible for us to store food correctly. Dishes we make with care and love, not only because we have to eat but also because it gives us pleasure, undeniably have a different energy, and it feels like a great achievement when we provide food that gives us instant gratification!

## HAZELNUT AND CINNAMON SMOOTHIE

4

Easy

5 minutes

4 days
in the fridge

- 1 1/2 cups (200 g) hazelnuts, peeled and toasted
- 4 1/4 cups (1 l) water
- 2 1/4 tbsp (50 g) wildflower honey
- ground cinnamon

Soak the hazelnuts in water overnight before making the smoothie. Drain the hazelnuts, put them in a blender, and gradually add the water they were soaked in. Blend until the mixture is smooth and has a uniform consistency.

If you prefer a smooth drink without bits, strain the smoothie with a fine mesh strainer, and then sweeten to taste. If, on the other hand, you prefer it with bits, leave it as it is, add the honey, and transfer it to a glass bottle.

Remember to shake the bottle before serving. Sprinkle with cinnamon, and serve with cookies for dipping.

BREAKFAST

# APPLE AND GINGER JUICE

4

Easy

10 minutes

30 minutes

4 days
in the fridge

- 4 apples
- 2 oz (50 g) ginger
- the juice of 2 lemons
- 1/4 cup (50 g) granulated sugar

Trim and wash the apples and ginger, then cut them into small pieces.

Dissolve the sugar in 4 1/4 cups (1 l) of water, bring to a boil, and then add the ginger, apples, and lemon juice. Boil for 30 minutes, then blend.
If you prefer clear juice, strain the liquid with a fine mesh strainer; if not, leave the juice as it is.

Remember to shake the bottle before drinking.

If you want to keep the juice for a longer period of time, divide it between glass jars, put the lids on, and boil them for 20 minutes until they vacuum seal.

BREAKFAST

# CHOCOLATE AND RASPBERRY MOUSSE

2

Easy

5 minutes

- 1 1/2 cups (300 g) hazelnut smoothie (see recipe on p. 58)
- 3 tbsp (30 g) unsweetened cocoa powder
- 2 1/2 tbsp (30 g) granulated sugar
- 4 1/4 tsp (15 g) potato flour
- 1/2 tbsp (10 g) dark chocolate chips
- 1/2 cup (100 g) raspberries
- 2 sprigs mint for decorating

5 minutes

1 day
in the fridge

Put the potato flour, cocoa powder, and sugar in a pan, mix thoroughly, and then gradually add the hazelnut smoothie. Bring to a boil, stirring continuously, then take off the heat and pour into two individual portion containers.

Wash the raspberries, and leave them to drain on a tea towel.

When the mousse is tepid, or cold, decorate with the chocolate chips, raspberries, and mint, put the lids on the containers, and keep in the refrigerator.

# DARK CHOCOLATE MEDALLIONS WITH ALMONDS AND SEEDS

4

Easy

15 minutes

10 minutes

6 days

- 14 oz (400 g) dark chocolate
- 2 tbsp (20 g) sliced almonds
- 1 1/2 tbsp (20 g) toasted rice
- 2 3/4 tbsp (20 g) pumpkin seeds
- 1 1/2 tbsp (20 g) brown sugar

Melt the chocolate over a bain-marie. When it's soft, smooth, and liquid, use a teaspoon to form small medallions on a piece of parchment paper. Top with a few sliced almonds, and leave to cool.

Dissolve the sugar in a pan with a tablespoon of water, stir until it browns, and then take off the heat. Add a few drops of caramel to each of the medallions, and then top with the toasted rice and seeds.

You can store the medallions for several days in a container, wrapped in tissue paper.

## WHITE CHOCOLATE WITH MUESLI

4

- 10.5 oz (300 g) white chocolate
- 2 tbsp pouring cream
- 1 1/4 cups (200 g) muesli of your choice

Easy

Melt the white chocolate over a bain-marie, add the cream, and mix until smooth, soft, and liquid.

10 minutes

Line a rimmed baking tray with parchment paper, and cover with muesli. Pour the chocolate on top, level out the mixture using a spatula, and leave to cool.

When the chocolate has hardened, break it up with a spatula or by hand, put the pieces in an airtight container, and keep in a cool, dry place.

5 days

# TANGERINE FLAVORED CHESTNUT FLOUR PANCAKES WITH ALMONDS

2

Easy

10 minutes

- 1 cup (100 g) chestnut flour
- 3/4 cup (2 dl) almond milk
- 1 egg
- the rind of 1 organic tangerine
- 1 tbsp (20 g) honey
- 2 3/4 tbsp (20 g) sliced almonds
- 2 tbsp peanut oil

5 minutes

3 days

Chop the tangerine rind. Mix the chestnut flour with the almond milk and the egg.

When the mixture is smooth and has a uniform consistency, add a little tangerine peel (leave about half of it aside) and some of the almonds. Heat a non-stick frying pan on the stove for a few seconds, grease the bottom and the edges using a bit of paper towel dipped in peanut oil, then pour in a ladleful of the batter. As soon as the pancake comes away from the pan, turn it over, and cook in the same way. Repeat until you have used all the batter.

Leave the pancakes to cool, then put them in a container with the remaining tangerine rind.

Before serving, decorate with the remaining almonds and sweeten with honey to taste.

# TANGERINE JELLY TART

4

Medium

15 minutes

30 minutes

- 2 1/4 cups (200 g) all-purpose flour
- 4 egg yolks
- 1/2 cup (100 g) granulated sugar
- 1/2 cup (100 g) soft butter
- 7 oz (200 g) tangerine jelly

Mix the flour, eggs, sugar, and butter without kneading, so as not to warm the dough. When the dough is compact, divide it into two pieces: a large one, and a smaller one for the decoration.

Preheat the oven to 350°F (180°C).

Roll out the base with a rolling pin, place it on a piece of paper, cut out a rectangle, and put it on a suitably sized baking tray.
Cover with the jelly. With the leftover pastry, make the decorations you want to put on the tart, and place them on top of the jelly. Bake in the oven for about 30 minutes, checking every now and then that it is cooking evenly.

Once the pastry is golden brown, take the tart out of the oven, and leave to cool. Cut it into squares, put them in paper molds, and put them in a box.

Presenting the tart like this is an excellent idea for giving your work colleagues a treat at coffee time.

# CHICKEN MEDALLIONS WITH MIXED CRUNCHY VEGETABLES

4

Easy

10 minutes

For the medallions:
- 7 oz (200 g) minced chicken
- 1/2 cup (50 g) Parmigiano Reggiano
- 2 eggs
- 1/2 cup (50 g) finely chopped dry bread
- 1/2 cup (50 g) all-purpose flour
- 3 1/2 tbsp (0.5 dl) peanut oil
- salt and pepper

For the vegetables:
- 1 1/4 cups (200 g) Romanesco broccoli
- 1/2 cup (100 g) daikon
- 1 carrot
- 1/2 bell pepper
- 1 1/4 cup (100 g) eggplant
- 2 tbsp extra virgin olive oil

10 minutes

5 days
in the fridge

Mix all of the ingredients for the medallions, except for the all-purpose flour, which you put on a plate. Add salt and pepper to taste. Mix until the mixture has a uniform consistency. With slightly damp hands, make the medallions, and then roll them in the flour.

Fry them in very hot oil for about 2 minutes on each side, then put them on a paper towel.

Trim the vegetables, cut into pieces, or be creative, and cook in a non-stick frying pan with extra virgin olive oil. Add salt and pepper during cooking.

If you like your vegetables crunchy, cook over medium heat for about 10 minutes, adding a little water when necessary, and once cooked add the medallions.

INDIVIDUAL PORTIONS

# TROFIE WITH BASIL AND ALMOND PESTO

4

Easy

20 minutes

10 minutes

2 days
in the fridge

- 14 oz (400 g) fresh trofie
- 5 sun-dried tomatoes
- 20 whole almonds
- 10 capers packed in salt
- 1 1/2 cup (30 g) basil leaves
- 1/2 cup (50 g) sweet mature pecorino, grated
- salt and pepper
- basil leaves for decorating

Finely chop the tomatoes, capers, and almonds (set aside 10 for decorating), and put them in a bowl. Finely chop the basil and add it to the other ingredients. Add the cheese and oil, then mix thoroughly. Add salt and pepper.

You can keep the sauce in a jar in the freezer, or for a few days in the refrigerator, with the lid on.

Cook the trofie in salted water, a few minutes less than indicated on the packet, then drain and rinse with cold water. Stir in the pesto, and keep in a glass jar, or in a microwave safe container with a lid.

Before serving, heat as much as you like, and decorate with the fresh basil.

INDIVIDUAL PORTIONS

# MIXED VEGETABLE AND TOFU CURRY

4

Easy

10 minutes

15 minutes

5 days
vacuum-packed

- 7 oz (200 g) tofu
- 2 zucchinis
- 1 eggplant
- 1 bell pepper
- 2 tbsp extra virgin olive oil
- 1 tbsp curry powder
- salt

Dice the tofu. Trim all of the vegetables, cut them into pieces, and steam for about 10 minutes until they are tender but still firm. Don't throw the cooking water away. Pour the oil into a non-stick frying pan, and dissolve the curry in a ladleful of the vegetable stock obtained from cooking the vegetables.

Cook the vegetables and tofu over high heat, adding a little curry stock every now and then, until they are the desired consistency.

The curried vegetables can be kept in vacuum sealed jars for up to 5 days, or in the freezer.

INDIVIDUAL PORTIONS

# SQUID SALAD WITH BROCCOFLOWER, BELL PEPPER, AND LEMON

2

Easy

5 minutes

- 14 oz (400 g) squid, cleaned
- 2 cups (300 g) broccoflower
- 2 bell peppers
- 2 spring onions
- 2 small tomatoes
- 1 lemon
- 2 tbsp extra virgin olive oil
- salt and pepper

5 minutes

1 day
in the fridge

Trim, wash, and drain the vegetables, cut them however you like, and put them in a bowl.

Steam the squid, and remove from the heat as soon as they change color (they turn white and curl up), so they don't become rubbery. Cut them into slices, and immediately dress them with oil, freshly squeezed lemon juice, salt, and pepper.

Add the squid to the vegetables, mix, and transfer to an airtight container.

Keep in the refrigerator.

To bring out the flavors in the salad, put it in a tepid bowl 30 minutes before serving.

INDIVIDUAL PORTIONS

# MILLET SALAD WITH BABY MOZZARELLAS AND VEGETABLES

2

Medium

20 minutes

3 days
in the fridge

- 1 1/4 cups (200 g) cooked millet
- 8 baby mozzarellas
- 12 cherry tomatoes
- 1 cucumber
- 1 lemon
- 1 small avocado
- 2 sprigs of basil, washed and dried
- 2–3 tbsp oil
- salt and pepper

Wash the cherry tomatoes, and cut them in half or into quarters, depending on their size. Put them in a container with the millet and baby mozzarellas, cut however you like.

Wash the cucumber and slice it lengthwise, then prepare the basil leaves.

Line an airtight container with a paper towel, then put the cucumber slices and basil inside. Put the lid on, and put in the refrigerator.

Mix the millet and the vegetables, pour into an airtight container, put the lid on, and keep in the refrigerator.

The salad can be kept in the refrigerator for 3 days.

Before serving, add the avocado (sliced or diced), oil, salt, pepper, and lemon juice. Arrange the cucumber slices around the inside edge of a 4-in (10 cm) ring mold. Use the slices to make a base, and fill with the salad. Decorate with the basil, remove the ring mold, and serve.

# VEGETABLE SOUP

2

Easy

10 minutes

40 minutes

7 days
frozen

- 1 potato
- 1 round zucchini
- 3/4 cup (100 g) celeriac
- 1 onion
- 3 1/3 cups (100 g) collard greens
- 10 cherry tomatoes
- 1 carrot
- 2 tbsp extra virgin olive oil
- salt and pepper
- slices of stale turmeric bread (optional)

Trim and wash all the vegetables, cut them into pieces, and put in a pan with 4 1/4 cups (1 l) of water. Boil for about 40 minutes, until they are soft. Add salt and pepper to taste before taking off the heat.

Leave to cool, put in a container, and keep in the freezer.

Take it out of the freezer a few hours before you need it, and then heat it on the stove for a few minutes. Serve with slices of turmeric bread and a drizzle of extra virgin olive oil.

# ORANGE CREAM DESSERT

2

Easy

10 minutes

6 days
vacuum-packed
in the fridge

- 2 organic oranges
- 4 oz (100 g) dry butter cookies
- 1/2 cup (100 g) ricotta
- 1/2 cup (100 g) mascarpone
- 3 tbsp (20 g) powdered sugar
- 1 tbsp rum (optional)

Put the ricotta, mascarpone, rum, and powdered sugar in a bowl, and mix with a whisk. Continue until the ingredients are thoroughly mixed.

Using a mortar and pestle, crush the cookies until they are tiny, uneven crumbs. Wet them with the juice of half an orange. Line the bottom of 4 small dishes with the cookies, and pour in the mascarpone cream. Decorate the desserts with orange slices, however you like.

Put the dishes in vacuum sealer bags, remove the air, and put the desserts in the refrigerator.

INDIVIDUAL PORTIONS

# ZUCCHINI AND CARROT NOODLES
# WITH BLACK RICE

4

Easy

10 minutes

2 days
in the fridge

- 2 zucchinis
- 1 carrot
- 1/2 cup (100 g) cooked black rice
- 1 small red bell pepper
- 10 baby mozzarellas
- 4 tbsp extra virgin olive oil
- 1 bunch of aromatic herbs (thyme, sage, marjoram)
- edible flowers (violets, daisies, etc.)
- salt and pepper

If you want the flowers and herbs you have bought to stay fresh for a few days, carefully wrap them in damp paper towels, without squashing them, and put them in a container with the lid on.

Wash the vegetables, and use a spiralizer, a mandoline, or a peeler — or any other tool you have — to make the zucchini and carrot noodles.

Trim and thinly slice the bell pepper.

Put the noodles in a bowl, add the baby mozzarellas, rice, bell pepper, oil, and salt and pepper to taste, then mix.

Transfer to an airtight container, and leave in the refrigerator to rest.

Take it out of the refrigerator a few hours before you need it. Mix before serving, and decorate with the aromatic herbs and flowers.

SNACKS

# VEGGIE PATTIES WITH APPLE SALAD

4

Easy

10 minutes

- 3 1/3 cups (100 g) borage or spinach, cooked and drained
- 1/4 cup (20 g) all-purpose flour
- 1/2 cup (1 dl) milk
- 1/4 cup (50 g) ricotta
- 1/2 cup (1 dl) peanut oil
- 3 1/3 cups (100 g) leaf vegetables
- 1 apple
- 2 tbsp extra virgin olive oil
- 4 tbsp lemon juice
- salt and pepper

10 minutes

1 day
in the fridge

If you want to preserve leaf vegetables for a few days, the best way is to trim, wash, and dry them, wrap them in a damp cloth, and then put them in a plastic bag, or a tightly closed container. This way you can keep them in the refrigerator for 4–5 days.

Finely chop the borage or spinach, then add the ricotta, milk, and flour; mix until you get a uniform consistency, then add salt and pepper to taste.

Heat the oil in a non-stick frying pan. When it's hot, add dollops of the mixture using a tablespoon. Cook for a couple of minutes, turn them over, and take them out of the pan when they are firm. Leave to drain on a paper towel.

When they have cooled down, wrap them in a paper towel and put them in a container. Before serving, heat the patties, slice the apple, and arrange the slices in a bowl with the salad. Dress with lemon juice and serve.

SNACKS

# RICE NOODLE PATTIES WITH COLLARD GREENS

4

Easy

5 minutes

10 minutes

4 days
in the fridge

- 7 oz (200 g) rice noodles
- 3 1/3 cups (100 g) small collard greens
- 2 spring onions
- 2 eggs
- 2 tbsp all-purpose flour
- 1/2 cup (1 dl) peanut oil
- 1/2 cup (1 dl) soy sauce

Trim and finely chop the collard greens; wash the spring onions, and finely chop one of them.

Cook the rice noodles in salted water, following the cooking time indicated on the packet (a couple of minutes are usually enough), and then drain them. Put them in a bowl, and stir in the collard greens and chopped spring onion. Add the eggs and flour, and mix thoroughly until the mixture has a uniform consistency. If it makes it easier, cut the noodles with a pair of scissors.

Heat the oil to about 325°F (170°C), then add dollops of the mixture using a tablespoon. Cook for a couple of minutes on each side. When they are a light golden brown, take them out of the pan and place on a paper towel to absorb any excess oil.

Keep the patties in a tightly closed container, wrapped in paper towels, until you are ready to use them.

Take the patties out of the refrigerator a few hours before you need them. Before serving, slice the remaining spring onion and add it to the soy sauce, which is served on the side.

SNACKS

# Week 3

When planning batch meals, only cooked dishes usually spring to mind, and actually it is easier to preserve the final product. However, if you want to use fresh leaf vegetables or flowers, without having to run out to the grocery store, it is good to know how to protect the tender leaves from rotting or oxidation.

First of all, you should buy only very fresh leaf vegetables, and after trimming them, they must be washed with the head intact. Once drained, they should be gently wrapped in a cotton towel and — being careful not to crush them — put in a container and then stored in the refrigerator. This way you will always have leaf vegetables on hand to add a touch of freshness to your dishes. The same applies to flowers, although delicate petals should be touched as little as possible, so instead of wrapping them in something, it is better to place them on wet paper towels in a well-sealed container, and then put them in the refrigerator.

You can also store delicate fruits, such as raspberries, in the same way, although the paper towels must be dry so that they can absorb any liquids and prevent fermentation. However, they can't be kept for very long: a maximum of 3–4 days. The same measures also apply to vegetables for salads. After washing them, it is best to wrap them in food grade paper, and keep them in separate containers so that they do not absorb the aromas of other foods. If you only use part of a tomato, cucumber, lemon, and so on, you should always put the leftover pieces in an airtight container so that they remain fresh for a few days.

# CARAMEL BLANCMANGE WITH HAZELNUTS AND ALMONDS

4

Easy

10 minutes

- 2 1/4 cups (5 dl) hot milk
- 1/4 cup (50 g) granulated sugar
- 1/2 tsp (2 g) powdered gelatin
- 2 tbsp unsweetened hazelnut paste
- 5 dry butter cookies
- 2 tbsp (10 g) sliced almonds

10 minutes

3 days
in the fridge

Soak the gelatin in cold water.

Caramelize the sugar in a pan that is big enough to add the milk. When it starts to smoke and has become a caramel-colored liquid, add the milk and stir into the liquid until blended. Stir in the hazelnut paste, turn off the heat, add the gelatin, and mix until completely dissolved.

Finely chop the cookies.

Divide the mixture between 4 single serving molds, leave to cool, and then decorate the blancmanges with the chopped cookies and sliced almonds.

Keep the desserts in the refrigerator, covered either with a silicone stretch lid or aluminum foil.

# SPICED PEARS IN MOSCATO WINE

4

Easy

5 minutes

40 minutes

2 days

- 8 Madernassa pears or similar cooking pears
- 4 1/4 cups (1 l) Moscato dessert wine
- 1 cinnamon stick
- 1 tbsp organic orange and tangerine rind
- 1 lemon

Wash the pears and stand them close together in a pan, with the stem ends up. Add the citrus rind, lemon juice, cinnamon, and wine.

Boil over medium heat with the lid on for about 40 minutes, turning the heat down if too much liquid is evaporating. Take off the heat and leave to cool, with the lid on.

If you want to preserve the pears, transfer them to hot airtight jars as soon as you have removed them from the heat: this will allow the jar to create a vacuum.

# DIPPING COOKIES

4

Easy

10 minutes

20 minutes

7 days

- 2 1/2 cups (300 g) all-purpose flour
- 2 eggs
- 1/2 cup (100 g) soft butter
- 1/2 cup (1 dl) milk
- 1/4 cup (50 g) granulated sugar
- 2 tsp (5 g) cake yeast
- 1/3 cup (100 g) jelly of your choice for decorating

Mix all the ingredients together until you have a smooth dough with a uniform consistency.

Wrap the dough in a tea towel, and leave to rest for a few hours. Preheat the oven to 350°F (180°C), then line a baking tray with parchment paper.

Roll out the dough on a smooth surface, to a thickness of about 0.5 in (1.5 cm). Cut out the cookies in any shape you like: flowers, discs, sticks, squares. Decorate some of them with the jelly.

Put the cookies on the baking tray, and bake for about 15–20 minutes. If you want some of them to have a darker color, sprinkle them with sugar before putting them in the oven, and bake them for 5 minutes longer.

You can keep the cookies in the pantry for a long time if you put them in a glass airtight jar or tin, or wrapped in tissue paper in a cardboard box.

# SWEET BREAD WITH MIXED BERRIES
# AND FRUIT JUICE

4

Easy

10 minutes

35 minutes

4 days
in the fridge

- 3 cups (300 g) whole wheat pastry flour
- 2 tsp (5 g) brewer's yeast
- 1/3 cup (50 g) blueberries
- 1/3 cup (50 g) strawberries
- 1 lemon
- 3 1/4 tbsp (20 g) dried cranberries
- 3 tbsp (20 g) powdered sugar

Trim the fruit and blend half of them together with freshly squeezed lemon juice. Pour the juice into an ice cube mold, and put it in the freezer.

Dissolve the yeast in 3/4 cup (2 dl) of warm water, then add the flour and stir until the mixture is lump-free. Add the remaining fresh and dry fruit. If the strawberries are big, cut them in half or into quarters. Cover the dough, then leave it to rise for at least 3 hours in a warm place.

Preheat the oven to 400°F (200°C), then line a baking tray with parchment paper. Divide the dough into small pieces, form them into any shape you like, and place them on the baking tray. Bake in the oven for 20 minutes, then turn them over and cook for another 15 minutes.

Leave to cool, put them in an airtight container, and keep them in the refrigerator.

Before serving, warm in the oven for 5 minutes at 400°F (200°C), then sprinkle with powdered sugar. Remove the fruit juice cubes from the freezer, blend them with 3/4 cup (2 dl) of water, and serve with the bread.

BREAKFAST

# ROSEMARY FLATBREAD

4

Easy

10 minutes

15 minutes

* 3 cups (300 g) whole wheat high gluten flour
* 0.7 oz (20 g) chopped rosemary
* 2 tbsp extra virgin olive oil
* 2 tsp (5 g) brewer's yeast
* salt

5 days

Put the flour on a work surface, dissolve the yeast in warm water (about 3/4 cup/2 dl), and mix into the flour. If necessary, add more water until you get the desired consistency. Add the rosemary and salt to taste, and continue to knead until the dough is smooth and elastic. Cover, and leave to rest in a warm place for about 2 hours.

Preheat the oven to 400°F (200°C), then line a baking tray with parchment paper. Divide the dough into pieces, and roll them into rectangles with a rolling pin. Bake the flatbreads for 10 minutes, turn them over, and cook for another 5 minutes.

Leave to cool, then put the flatbreads in a paper bag and store in a cool, dry place.

# APPLE AND DRIED FRUIT STRUDEL

2

Easy

10 minutes

20 minutes

2 days
in the fridge

- 9 oz (250 g) ready-made puff pastry
- 1 pear
- 1 apple
- 1 banana
- 1/3 cup (30 g) chopped hazelnuts
- 1 egg yolk

Roll out the pastry, leaving the parchment paper on so that it doesn't stick to the work surface. Divide it into 4 pieces.

Peel the fruit, then cut them into rounds and small pieces. Divide the fruit equally between the 4 pieces of pastry. Take half of the hazelnuts and sprinkle them on top of the fruit. Fold the pastry over the fruit, adapting to the shape of the pieces. Brush the top with egg yolk.

Preheat the oven to 350°F (180°C). Line a baking tray with parchment paper, then bake the strudels in the oven for 20 minutes. Check if they are golden brown and crispy, and if not, leave them to cook for a few more minutes.

Take out of the oven, leave to cool, and put in a container with a lid. Before serving, warm in the oven at 400°F (200°C) for 3–4 minutes.

# RICE AND COCONUT MILK CREPES
# WITH PEACH JELLY

4

Medium

10 minutes

- 3/4 cup (2 dl) coconut milk
- 2 eggs
- 2 tbsp rice flour
- 1 tbsp wheat flour
- 2 tbsp peach jelly
- 1 tbsp oil

10 minutes

Mix the coconut milk, eggs, and both flours. When the batter is smooth, heat a non-stick frying pan with a diameter of 8 in (20 cm).

1 day
in the fridge

Grease the frying pan using a bit of paper towel, pour in a ladleful of batter, and cook until it sets. Turn the crepe over, and cook for about 1 minute. Spread with jelly, then roll the crepe up. Repeat until the batter is finished.

Put the crepes in a container with a lid, making sure it is long enough for the crepes not to bend. Leave to rest in the refrigerator until you are ready to use them.

You can serve them with some extra jelly on the side.

# ROAST LITTLE TUNA WITH ARTICHOKES
# AND FRESH ORANGE SALAD

4

Easy

15 minutes

15 minutes

1 day
in the fridge

- 21 oz (600 g) little tuna fillets
- 4 artichokes
- 4 oz (100 g) trimmed chicory
- 2 organic oranges
- 1 lemon
- 4 tbsp extra virgin olive oil
- 4 tbsp white vinegar
- salt and pepper

Store the chicory in a cool place, wrapped in a damp cloth in an airtight container.

Trim the artichokes, remove any spiny or leathery parts, wash them, and then boil for 5 minutes (this will make them crunchy) in 2 1/4 cups (0.5 l) of water with the vinegar. Drain, then put them to one side until you need them.

Wash the little tuna fillets thoroughly, cut them into pieces, and marinate them in the juice of the lemon and one orange.
Pour the oil into a frying pan, and cook the fillets over medium heat, wetting them with the marinade. Add salt and pepper to taste, then add the artichokes, and leave to cook for 5–6 minutes.

Leave to cool, then transfer to an airtight container.

Before serving, heat the little tuna in a pan for 2 minutes. Slice half of the remaining orange, arrange the chicory and orange slices on a plate, followed by the artichokes with the little tuna on top. Squeeze the other half of the orange over the top.

INDIVIDUAL PORTIONS

# SMOKED SALMON PARCELS STUFFED WITH MIXED BERRIES

2

Easy

10 minutes

2 days
in the fridge

- 4 slices of smoked salmon
- 1 head of chicory
- 10 raspberries
- 10 blueberries
- 4 strawberries
- 1 lemon
- 2 tbsp extra virgin olive oil
- peppercorns

It is best to assemble this dish at the last moment, so that the various ingredients maintain their freshness and their individual flavors.

You can prepare the fruit, chicory, and salmon separately, and store them in different containers.

Trim the chicory leaves, and put them on a dishcloth. Wash the fruit carefully and leave them to dry on a tea towel. Wrap the chicory, without squashing the leaves, and put them in an airtight container. Do the same with the fruit.

Just before serving, put two or three chicory leaves, one strawberry, and a few blueberries and raspberries on the salmon slices, then roll them up. Arrange the salmon rolls on a plate with the salad and remaining fruit, then season with oil, pepper, and the freshly squeezed lemon juice.

INDIVIDUAL PORTIONS

# WHITE BEAN SALAD WITH BELUGA LENTILS

4

Easy

10 minutes

60 minutes

7 days
vacuum-packed

- 3/4 cup (150 g) navy beans
- 2 1/3 cups (450 g) beluga lentils
- 10 cherry tomatoes
- 1 spring onion
- 4 tbsp extra virgin olive oil
- 2 tbsp vinegar
- 2 dried chili peppers
- salt

Trim the spring onion and wash the cherry tomatoes.

Boil the beans and lentils separately in salted water. You need to drain them when they are tender but still compact, so keep checking them. Neither of the legumes needs to be soaked, but if you put them to soak (separately) the evening before cooking them, they will cook much faster: about 30 minutes for the beluga lentils, and 1 hour for the navy beans.

Once cooked, drain them and add the spring onion, tomatoes, crumbled chili peppers, salt, and oil. Transfer to a hot jar, put the lid on, cook over a bain-marie for 20 minutes, then leave to cool.

The vacuum-sealed jar will preserve the salad for a long time, even out of the refrigerator.

INDIVIDUAL PORTIONS

# PUMPKIN AND BARLEY BROTH

4

Easy

10 minutes

60 minutes

5 days
in the fridge

- 1 cup (200 g) pearl barley
- 11 oz (300 g) pumpkin
- 3 1/2 tbsp (50 g) butter
- 4 1/4 cups (1 l) vegetable stock
- 1/3 oz (10 g) fresh thyme
- salt
- pepper

Wash the barley repeatedly in cold water, then drain it. Trim the pumpkin and cut the flesh into small pieces. Boil it for 20 minutes in the vegetable stock.

Melt the butter in a pan, and lightly toast the barley. Use a perforated spoon to take the pumpkin out of the stock, and stir it into the barley. Cook for a few minutes, then start adding the stock a little at a time, continuing to do so until the ingredients are cooked; it should take about 40 minutes. Add salt and pepper to taste. Once cooked, add the thyme to give the dish a delicious aroma!

Put in an airtight glass jar, and keep in the refrigerator until you're ready to eat it.

INDIVIDUAL PORTIONS

# BELL PEPPERS STUFFED WITH GREEN PEPPER AND SOY SAUCE TOFU

4

Easy

10 minutes

- 4 red bell peppers
- 11 oz (300 g) tofu
- 1 boiled potato
- 1 eggplant
- 4 tbsp white vinegar
- 2 tbsp extra virgin olive oil
- green peppercorns
- 1 tbsp soy sauce
- salt

10 minutes

5 minutes

5 days
in the fridge

Wash the bell peppers, cut them in half, and create a kind of bowl for the filling. Boil in water and vinegar for 5 minutes, then drain, keeping the cooking water.

Dice the eggplant, then cook it in the saved cooking water for 5 minutes. Drain in a colander, then transfer to a bowl. Stir in the pieces of boiled potato. Add 7 oz (200 g) of finely chopped tofu to the eggplant and potato mixture. Season with salt, green pepper, and soy sauce.

Stuff the bell peppers, place them on a baking tray, top with slices of tofu, and cook in the oven, preheated to 400°F (200°C), for 5 minutes.

Take out of the oven, leave to cool, put in vacuum seal containers, and keep in the refrigerator.

INDIVIDUAL PORTIONS

## POTATO AND WALNUT SALAD

4

Easy

5 minutes

30 minutes

4 days
in the fridge

- 4 potatoes
- 1 carrot
- 1 3/4 cups (400 g) Greek yogurt

- 1/2 cup (50 g) shelled walnuts
- 1 3/4 tbsp (20 g) grated Parmigiano Reggiano
- salt and pepper

Wash the potatoes and the carrot, boil them for about 30 minutes, then drain and leave to cool.

Cut the vegetables into slices or pieces, add the walnut kernels, salt and pepper to taste, and, finally, the Greek yogurt. Mix all the ingredients, then divide the salad between single serving dishes. Vacuum seal, and then keep in the refrigerator.

Take them out of the refrigerator just before serving, and sprinkle them with the grated Parmigiano Reggiano.

INDIVIDUAL PORTIONS

## SEITAN AND VEGETABLE STIR FRY

4

Easy

5 minutes

10–15 minutes

3 days
in the fridge

- 11 oz (300 g) seitan
- 7 oz (200 g) pumpkin
- 1 small head of Swiss chard
- 10 pearl onions
- 4 baby bell peppers
- 2 tbsp extra virgin olive oil
- salt and pepper

Trim, wash, and dry the vegetables. Slice the pumpkin and the seitan, chop the Swiss chard, and cut the bell peppers into rounds. If the pearl onions are small, leave them whole.

Pour the oil into a pan, add the vegetables and the seitan, then season with salt and pepper. Fry the ingredients for 5 minutes over high heat, stirring continuously. Add a few tablespoons of water when needed, and cook until the ingredients reach the desired consistency (5–10 minutes should be enough).

Transfer to a microwave safe container.

INDIVIDUAL PORTIONS

# CAPER BREAD WITH VEGETABLE
# AND MAYONNAISE SPREAD

4

Easy

10 minutes

- 14 oz (400 g) bread dough (see recipe on p. 98)
- 2 1/4 tbsp (20 g) capers packed in salt
- 1 1/4 tsp (5 g) caper powder
- 3/4 cup (200 g) mayonnaise
- 2 carrots
- 3 1/2 tbsp (0.5 dl) apple cider vinegar
- pepper

3 minutes

Sift the capers to remove most of the salt, but don't wash them. Knead them into the bread dough, and then form small loaves.

25 minutes

Bake in the oven, preheated to 400°F (200°C), for about 15–20 minutes, then turn them over and leave them in the oven for another 5 minutes.

Meanwhile, trim the carrots and cut them into small sticks. Boil them in water and vinegar for 3 minutes, then drain them. When they are cold, add them to the mayonnaise. Season with pepper and caper powder. Do not add salt.

2 days

Put the carrot mayonnaise in a vacuum seal container, and keep in the refrigerator until you're ready to use it.

Before serving, warm the caper bread in the oven for 5 minutes to revive it, and serve with the carrot mayonnaise.

# SPECK ROLLS STUFFED WITH DATES AND ALMONDS

4

Easy

- 20 slices of speck
- 20 dates
- 20 almonds

5 minutes

3–4 minutes

Remove the stones from the dates.

Put the slices of speck on a smooth surface. Cover each slice with dates and almonds, then wrap the speck around the fruit to create little rolls.

4 days
in the fridge

Put the rolls in a container that will preserve their freshness and goodness, then put them in the refrigerator until you need them.

Before serving, heat a non-stick frying pan on the stove, and cook the rolls for 3–4 minutes, turning them continuously. Arrange them on a serving plate. Thanks to the heat, the various flavors will blend together, reducing the fatty part of the speck at the same time!

# WHOLE WHEAT BREAD ROLLS WITH PÂTÉ AND WALNUTS

4

Easy

15 minutes

30 minutes

1 day

**For the rolls:**
- 2 1/2 cups (250 g) whole wheat flour
- 2 tbsp (20 g) sesame seeds
- 2 tsp (5 g) baker's yeast
- salt

**For the filling:**
- 20 walnut kernels
- 3.5 oz (100 g) tuna in oil
- 2 tbsp raisin wine
- 2 tbsp (30 g) butter
- 20 shelled pumpkin seeds
- salt and pepper

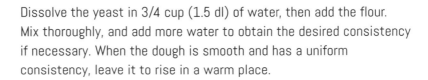

Dissolve the yeast in 3/4 cup (1.5 dl) of water, then add the flour. Mix thoroughly, and add more water to obtain the desired consistency if necessary. When the dough is smooth and has a uniform consistency, leave it to rise in a warm place.

Meanwhile, blend the tuna with the wine and butter. Roughly chop the pumpkin seeds, then add them to the tuna mixture. Season with salt and pepper. Put the pâté in an airtight container until you are ready to use it.

Preheat the oven to 350°F (180°C).

Roll the dough out with a rolling pin, then cut out 1/2-in (1 cm) thick discs using a ring mold. Leave the discs to rise on a baking tray lined with parchment paper. Sprinkle the top with sesame seeds, then leave to rest for 30 minutes. Bake in the oven for half an hour.

To serve, cut the rolls in half and fill with the pâté and walnut kernels.

SNACKS

# Week 4

Batch cooking is a great way to monitor meals and ensure our diet is varied, to decide whether we include nutrients beneficial to our well-being, and to make sure that healthy foods such as vegetables, fruits, carbohydrates, and proteins are well-distributed. We can also choose to use whole-grain carbohydrates or small amounts of sugar in our jellies. We can make dairy-free drinks with seeds and dried fruit, as well as enjoy a fun evening with friends without having to slave over the stove. All you need to do, for example, is take the lid off a container or transfer a healthy, tasty rice salad from a container into a salad bowl.

And what if there are leftovers? If there's some leftover rice salad, for example, there are several options: you can recycle it to make something else, such as croquettes, rice balls, or soup, or put it in a container and freeze it for those times when the refrigerator is bare!

And what if we want to stock up on jellies or juices? Jellies are really easy: just remember what your parents and grandparents used to do. Choose your fruit, decide how much sugar you want to add — a little, a lot, or somewhere in between — and once cooked, divide the jelly between the jars, put the lids on, and boil them for 20 minutes. Leave the jars in the water to cool down, allowing the lids to seal, and then keep the jars in a cool, dark place until you're ready to use them. What about juices? Once you've made the juice, you can pour it into ice cube molds and use it to make original aperitifs or into small vacuum-sealed bottles for the freezer.

# WHOLE WHEAT CROISSANTS WITH PLUM JELLY AND FRUIT JUICE

4

Easy

20 minutes

60 minutes

7 days

- 70 oz (2 kg) plums
- 1 1/2 cups (300 g) granulated sugar
- 4 plain whole wheat croissants

To make the juice, boil 17.5 oz (500 g) of pitted plums in 4 1/4 cups (1 l) of water with 1/2 cup (100 g) of sugar. Boil for 20 minutes, blend, and pour the liquid into hot airtight bottles, or into single-serve bottles of your choice.

In this way, the lid is sucked down onto the bottle, creating a vacuum. Otherwise, boil the filled bottles for 20 minutes.

To make the jelly, put the remaining pitted plums in a pan with the remaining granulated sugar. Cook over medium heat for about 1 hour, stirring every now and then, until the liquid has reduced and comes away from the pan. When the jelly is the desired consistency, take off the heat and immediately pour into boiling hot airtight glass jars.

Once they have vacuum sealed, you can store the jars of jelly in a cool place.

Serve the croissants at breakfast with the jelly and the plum juice.

# ALMOND AND DATE SMOOTHIE
# WITH BLUEBERRY BREAD

4

Easy

20 minutes

30 minutes

5 days
in the fridge

For the smoothie:
- 10 pitted dates
- 30 almonds

For the bread:
- 11 oz (300 g) ready-made bread dough
- 3/4 cup (100 g) blueberries
- 1 tbsp (10 g) flax seeds

To make the smoothie, blend the dates and almonds with 4 1/4 cups (1 l) of water. If you want the smoothie to be richer and more nutritious, you can use soya or oat milk instead of water, or any substitute you like.

Put the smoothie into any type of vacuum seal container, and keep it in the refrigerator.

Shake well before drinking to mix the solids with the liquid.

To make the bread, knead the blueberries into the dough, then form a loaf that will be easy to slice once cooked. Sprinkle with the flax seeds, then cook for about 30 minutes in the oven, preheated to 350°F (180°C). Use a toothpick to check if it's cooked: if it comes out clean, the bread's ready.

Put the bread in vacuum sealed bags, and keep in the refrigerator until you are ready to eat it. To revive the bread, put the whole loaf, or slices, in the oven at 400°F (200°C) for a few minutes before serving.

# CREAMY YOGURT AND RICOTTA
# WITH MIXED BERRIES

4

Easy

5 minutes

3 days
in the fridge

- 1 1/3 cups (300 g) Greek yogurt
- 3/4 cup (200 g) ricotta
- 2 tbsp honey
- 1 1/3 cups (200 g) mixed berries: red currants and blueberries

Trim and wash the fruit, then leave them to dry on a tea towel.
Put them in an airtight container wrapped in a paper towel, and keep in the refrigerator until you are ready to use them.

Mix the yogurt and ricotta with the honey, until smooth and creamy.

Put in an airtight container, and keep in the refrigerator until you are ready to eat it.

Before serving, divide between single serving dishes, and decorate with the mixed berries.

BREAKFAST

# FAT-FREE SPONGE CAKE

2

Easy

10 minutes

20–25 minutes

6 days

- 2 1/4 cups (200 g) all-purpose flour
- 3 eggs
- 1/2 cup (80 g) granulated sugar
- 3 tbsp (20 g) powdered sugar
- grated rind of 1 lemon

Separate the egg yolks from the whites. Whisk the egg yolks with the sugar until soft and light in color. Add the freshly grated lemon rind. In another bowl, whisk the egg whites until stiff.
Sift the flour into the egg yolk mixture, and mix thoroughly.
Finally, gently fold in the egg whites.

Preheat the oven to 320°F (160°C).

Line a baking tray with parchment paper and pour in the mixture. Bake in the oven for 20 minutes, then use a toothpick to check if it is cooked in the middle. If it comes out clean, the cake is ready, otherwise leave it in the oven for a few more minutes.

Once cooked, take it out of the oven, leave to cool, then put it in a cardboard box or a tin, wrapped in tissue paper.

Sprinkle with powdered sugar before serving.

# CHOCOLATE AND SESAME SEED DONUTS

2

Medium

10 minutes

20 minutes

![fridge icon]

4 days
in the fridge

- 2 1/4 cups (200 g) all-purpose flour
- 2 egg yolks
- 3 tbsp milk
- 1 tsp (2 g) cake yeast
- 7 oz (200 g) dark chocolate
- 3 1/4 tbsp (30 g) sesame seeds

Mix the flour with the egg yolks, yeast, and milk, until you have a smooth, shiny dough.

Roll the dough out, then cut out 1/2-in (1 cm) thick discs using a ring mold; use a smaller ring mold to make the holes in the middle.

Melt the chocolate over a bain-marie. Pour the sesame seeds onto a plate.

Preheat the oven to 350°F (180°C). Put the donuts on a baking tray lined with parchment paper, and cook for 20 minutes. When they have risen and are golden brown, take them out of the oven, and leave to cool. Dip the donuts in the melted chocolate, then in the sesame seeds.

Put the donuts in an airtight container and keep in the refrigerator. Take them out 1 hour before serving, and leave at room temperature.

# MILK RICE WITH FRESH STRAWBERRIES AND ZUCCHINI

4

Easy

5 minutes

12 minutes

1 day
in the fridge

- 1 cup (200 g) basmati rice
- 1 small zucchini
- 3/4 cup (100 g) strawberries
- 2 1/4 cups (5 dl) milk
- 3 1/2 tbsp (50 g) butter
- 2 sage leaves
- salt and pepper

Trim the strawberries and cut them in half, or into quarters, depending on their size. Wash the zucchini and cut it into noodles. Melt the butter in a non-stick pan. Heat the milk and then keep it warm until you need it.

Toast the rice in the butter, add the sage leaves, zucchini, and strawberries. As soon as the liquid evaporates, start adding the milk a little at a time. Season with salt and pepper, or keep it sweet if you prefer. Cook over low heat, stirring continuously while you add the milk.

When the rice reaches the desired consistency (basmati rice cooks in about 12 minutes), take off the heat and divide between single serving dishes.

Keep in the refrigerator until you are ready to serve it.

You can either serve the rice cold — great in summer — or at room temperature.

# PARMIGIANO REGGIANO BREADSTICKS WITH RICOTTA AND SESAME SEED DIP

4

Easy

10 minutes

15 minutes

2 days
in the fridge

For the dip:
- 3/4 cup (200 g) ricotta
- 1/2 cup (100 g) mascarpone
- 2 tbsp (20 g) sesame seeds

For the breadsticks:
- 2 1/4 cups (200 g) all-purpose flour
- 2 tbsp extra virgin olive oil
- 1 3/4 tbsp (20 g) grated Parmigiano Reggiano

Preheat the oven to 350°F (180°C).

Mix the flour with 1/2 cup (1 dl) of water until you have a shiny, elastic dough with a uniform consistency. Leave to rest in a warm place for several hours, 24 hours if possible.

Divide the dough into pieces, and roll them into a sausage shape. If you like, you can twist them to form a kind of spiral. Place them on a baking tray lined with parchment paper, then sprinkle them with the grated cheese. Bake in the oven for 15 minutes, then leave to cool.

To make the dip, crush the sesame seeds using a mortar and pestle, then add the ricotta and mascarpone. Mix until smooth and creamy.

Put the dip in an airtight container, and keep in the refrigerator until you are ready to use it.

BREAKFAST

# PAPPARDELLE WITH MUSSEL AND CLAM SAUCE

4

Easy

5 minutes

12–15 minutes

7 days
frozen

- 11 oz (300 g) fresh pappardelle
- 18 oz (500 g) mussels
- 18 oz (500 g) clams
- 1 tbsp (20 g) parsley
- 1 clove of garlic
- 4 tbsp extra virgin olive oil
- salt and pepper

Trim, wash, dry, and chop the parsley. Wash the mussels and clams, then make them open in a frying pan, without any additional liquid. They are cooked inside when the valves open. Take off the heat and remove the shells. Strain the cooking juices and put it to one side.

Put the oil in a pan with the garlic, and brown for 1 minute over high heat. Add the shelled mollusks, flavor with parsley, season with salt and pepper, and add a couple of tablespoons of the cooking juices. Take off the heat and cover.

Boil the pappardelle in a large pan of salted water, cooking it for a couple of minutes less than the time indicated on the packet. Drain and pour into the sauce; leave it to cool.

Pour the pasta into a container with a lid, and put in the freezer.

Remove from the freezer the day before, and heat the pasta in a frying pan with a couple of tablespoons of oil.

# FRIED SNOW PEAS WITH CEREAL PATTIES

2

Easy

10 minutes

15 minutes

*
3 days
in the fridge

- 1/2 cup (100 g) cooked brown rice
- 1/2 cup (100 g) cranberry beans, cooked and shelled
- 1 egg
- 11 oz (300 g) snow peas
- 1 clove of garlic
- 4 tbsp extra virgin olive oil
- salt and pepper

Blend the beans with half of the brown rice, then add the remaining rice and the egg; add salt and pepper to taste. Put 2 tablespoons of oil on a plate.

Line a baking tray with parchment paper, and preheat the oven to 400°F (200°C). Roll out the mixture between two sheets of parchment paper. Cut out discs using a ring mold with a diameter of about 2 1/2 in (6 cm), dip them in the oil, and place them on the baking tray.

Put in the oven and cook for about 15 minutes, turning them over halfway through.

Meanwhile, trim, wash, and cut the snow peas. Put the remaining oil in a non-stick frying pan with the garlic, and add the snow peas. Fry for 5 minutes, then season with salt and pepper.

Keep the snow peas and patties in the refrigerator, in two separate airtight containers.

INDIVIDUAL PORTIONS

# COD WITH MUSHROOMS AND RED CABBAGE SALAD

4

Easy

10 minutes

10 minutes

2 days
in the fridge

- 21 oz (600 g) cod steaks
- 12 dried mushrooms
- 4 carrots
- 4 spring onions
- 11 oz (300 g) red cabbage
- 1 bell pepper
- 4 fresh sage leaves

- 4 tbsp extra virgin olive oil
- 2 tbsp soy sauce
- 1 tbsp vinegar
- 2 cloves of garlic
- 1 tsp freshly grated
  ginger
- salt and pepper

Soak the mushrooms in warm water. Trim the cabbage and the carrots. Wash the vegetables, julienne the carrots, and thinly slice the bell pepper and red cabbage. Put the cabbage in a bowl and dress with one sliced clove of garlic, 1 tablespoon of oil, vinegar, and salt and pepper to taste. Mix the salad and put in an airtight container. Keep in the refrigerator until you are ready to use it.

When the mushrooms have softened, cut them into pieces. Cut the spring onions into slices or rounds. Put the oil, remaining garlic, mushrooms, onions, carrots, and bell pepper in a frying pan. Stir the ingredients and cook them for 5 minutes, adding boiling water when necessary.

Cut the cod steaks into pieces, and add to the frying pan with the soy sauce and ginger. Cook over high heat until cooked (about 5 minutes), adding spoonfuls of water when necessary. Season with pepper (don't add salt because the soy sauce has a very strong flavor).

Remove from the heat, leave to cool, and store in airtight containers.

Before serving, heat the dish in a frying pan or in the microwave. Serve with the red cabbage salad, at room temperature, and decorate with the sage leaves.

INDIVIDUAL PORTIONS

# MEZZE MANICHE PASTA WITH OLIVES AND CHILI PEPPER SAUCE

2

Easy

2 minutes

10 minutes

5 days
frozen

- 7 oz (200 g) mezze maniche pasta
- 2 oz (50 g) olives
- 1 tbsp harissa chili paste
- 4 tbsp extra virgin olive oil
- 4 dried chili peppers
- 1 clove of garlic

Pour the oil into a non-stick frying pan, dissolve the harissa, and add the garlic. Crumble in the dried chili peppers, and add the drained olives. Stir and cook over high heat for 2–3 minutes to release all the flavors, then turn off and cover.

Cook the pasta in a generous amount of salted water, taking it off the heat 2 minutes before the cooking time indicated on the packet. Drain, pour the pasta into the sauce, mix, and leave to cool with the lid on.

Transfer to a container with a lid, and keep in the freezer. Remove from the freezer and put it in the refrigerator the day before you need it.

Heat the pasta in the microwave, or in a frying pan if you prefer it a little crunchier and more browned.

# MIXED STUFFED VEGETABLES

4

Easy

10 minutes

- 2 zucchinis
- 2 bell peppers
- 2 eggplants
- 1/2 cup (100 g) rice
- 1/4 cup (50 g) lentils
- 1/2 cup (50 g) Parmigiano Reggiano
- 4 tbsp extra virgin olive oil
- salt and pepper

18 minutes

Preheat the oven to 400°F (200°C).

Boil the rice and lentils together in 3 cups of water. Cook over low heat with the lid on until all the water has been absorbed; leave to rest. Stir in 2 tablespoons of oil and half of the cheese; add salt and pepper to taste.

20 minutes

Trim the vegetables, which you can substitute depending on the season (pumpkin, tomato, etc.). Scoop out the flesh, brush with oil, and stuff them with the rice mixture.

Cook in the oven for about 20 minutes, leave to cool, and then put them in a freezer safe container.

6 days
frozen

Take them out of the freezer and put in the refrigerator the day before you need them. Before serving, sprinkle with Parmigiano Reggiano and heat them under the grill.

INDIVIDUAL PORTIONS

# MIXED SALAD WITH CHICKEN ROLLS

2

Easy

10 minutes

20 minutes

4 days
in the fridge

- 5 oz (150 g) mixed leaf vegetables and edible flowers
- 11 oz (300 g) sliced chicken breast
- 1 zucchini
- 4–6 sage leaves
- 2 tbsp extra virgin olive oil
- salt and pepper

Preheat the oven to 400°F (200°C), and line a baking tray with parchment paper.

Slice the zucchini with a mandoline. Put the ribbons on top of the chicken slices, add the sage, and then roll them up. Add salt and pepper to taste. Put them on a baking tray and cook in the oven for 20 minutes, turning them over halfway through.

Trim, wash, and drain the leaf vegetables, then wrap them in a tea towel and put them in an airtight container until you are ready to use them.

Once cooked, leave the chicken rolls to cool, put them in an airtight container, and keep them in the refrigerator until you need them.

Before serving, arrange the salad on a serving plate, cut the chicken rolls into slices, and season with oil, salt, and pepper.

INDIVIDUAL PORTIONS

# WHEAT SALAD WITH GREEN SALAD

4

Easy

10 minutes

- 1 cup (200 g) whole wheat berries
- 2 tomatoes
- 1 head of endive
- 4 tbsp extra virgin olive oil
- 1 lemon
- 1 tbsp capers packed in vinegar
- salt and pepper

40 minutes

![fridge icon]

1 day
in the fridge

When you have leftovers, you can reuse them or add them to something else, such as a wheat salad.

Wash the wheat, and boil it in salted water for 40 minutes, then drain. If you want to preserve it, you can put it in vacuum sealed jars to have a supply of it whenever you need it.

Trim, wash, and drain the endive, wrap it in a damp tea towel and keep it in a plastic bag until you are ready to use it.

Before serving, arrange the salad on a serving plate and add the sliced tomatoes. Mix the wheat with your leftovers, and dress with the capers, oil, and freshly squeezed lemon juice. Serve at room temperature.

INDIVIDUAL PORTIONS

# SALTED FRITTERS WITH VEGETABLE SALAD

4

Easy

10 minutes

10 minutes

2 days
in the fridge

For the fritters:
- 2 1/4 cups (200 g) all-purpose flour
- 1 tsp (2 g) baker's yeast
- 2 tbsp extra virgin olive oil
- 1/2 cup (1 dl) peanut oil

For the salad:
- 3/4 cup (100 g) shelled peas
- 1 carrot
- 1 potato
- 3/4 cup (200 g) ready-made mayonnaise
- 2 tbsp apple cider vinegar
- salt and pepper

Peel the carrot and the potato, cut into small pieces, boil in salted water and vinegar for 5 minutes, then drain. Boil the peas for 10 minutes, and then mix all the vegetables together. Leave to cool, add the mayonnaise, and salt and pepper to taste.

Mix the flour with the yeast dissolved in 1/2 cup (1 dl) of water. When the mixture is smooth and elastic, flatten it and cut it into different sized strips.

Heat the oil, add the fritters, and fry until they have puffed up and are golden brown. Remove from the oil, drain on a paper towel, then add the salt.

Store the salad in a closed container in the refrigerator, and the fritters wrapped in tissue paper in a box.

SNACKS

# SHRIMP AND ZUCCHINI ROLLS

2

Medium

20 minutes

10 minutes

1 day
in the fridge

- 8 sheets of phyllo pastry
- 16 shelled shrimp
- 1 zucchini
- 16 basil leaves
- 2 tbsp extra virgin olive oil
- salt

Trim, wash, and dry the basil. Wash the zucchini, and cut it into thin slices (use a mandoline or a slicer). Cut the sheets of pastry in half, and fold each sheet over onto itself. Parboil the shrimp for 30 seconds, and drain them as soon as they change color: they go from translucent to pink.

Put a slice of zucchini, 2 shrimp, 2 basil leaves, salt, and pepper on each sheet of pastry, and close them firmly so the filling doesn't come out.

Line a baking tray with parchment paper, brush the rolls with oil, and put them on the baking tray. Cook in the oven for 5 minutes at 400°F (200°C), then turn them over and cook for another 5 minutes.

Keep them in a container lined with parchment paper.

Before serving, heat them in the oven for 2–3 minutes at 400°F (200°C).

SNACKS

# RED RICE AND CASHEW SALAD
# WITH AROMATIC HERBS

4

Easy

- 1 cup (200 g) red rice
- 1 carrot
- 2 sticks of celery
- 1/4 red bell pepper
- 1/4 yellow bell pepper
- 1 spring onion

- 1/4 cup (30 g) cashews
- 1 lemon
- 1 bunch of fresh aromatic herbs: thyme, marjoram, oregano
- extra virgin olive oil to taste
- salt and pepper

10 minutes

20 minutes

Cook the rice in 2 cups of salted water, and remove from the heat when the water has been absorbed; leave to cool.

4 days
in the fridge

Put the rice in a glass jar with the lid on.

Meanwhile, trim and cut the vegetables, then wrap each of them separately in a paper towel. Do the same with the herbs. Put them in an airtight container.

Before serving, mix all the ingredients together and dress with oil, salt, pepper, and freshly squeezed lemon.

# Index of Ingredients

# The Author

CINZIA TRENCHI is a naturopath, freelance journalist, and photographer specializing in nutrition and food and wine. She has contributed to numerous cookbooks published by both Italian and international publishers. She is a passionate cook, and for many years she has worked with various Italian publications, revisiting regional, traditional, and macrobiotic dishes, providing articles and photographs, as well as her own recipes. Her cookbooks contain original and creative diets, with unusual flavor combinations and pairings for creating new and delicious dishes, always taking into consideration the nutritional composition of foods to produce better balanced meals and, consequently, an improved state of well-being. She lives in the Piedmont countryside, in Monferrato, and uses the flowers, aromatic herbs, and vegetables in her garden to make innovative sauces and condiments, as well as decorations for her dishes. She always allows herself to be guided by the evolution of the season and her knowledge of the fruits of the earth. In recent years, she has written several titles for White Star with enthusiasm and creativity.

WHITE STAR PUBLISHERS

WS White Star Publishers® is a registered trademark property of White Star s.r.l.

© 2021 White Star s.r.l.
Piazzale Luigi Cadorna, 6
20123 Milan, Italy
www.whitestar.it

ISBN 978-88-544-1745-8
1 2 3 4 5 6   25 24 23 22 21

Translation: TperTradurre s.r.l. - Editing: Abby Young

Printed in Serbia